Living Well
2nd Edition (colour)

An Ethics Guide for Adolescents and Adults

Andrew Piekarski

Copyright © 2019 Andrew Piekarski

All rights reserved.

ISBN:978-0-9940387-5-3

CONTENTS

Preface

1. What it Means and How to Do It 1
2. Nine Precepts for Living Well 11
3. Exercises 13
4. Endnotes and References 18

Preface

This booklet is based on one written for our children by my wife and me in June, 2011. Our 16-year old son had asked us to summarize, in one document, our beliefs on how one should live.

We had been nickel-and-diming our children with ethics since they were born, not always consistently. This forced us to think it all through, tie things together and fill in the gaps. By our measure, the book was an immediate success though its future effects remain to be evaluated.

Our children are now well on the way to adulthood. Adults usually require more background information, references and more "depth". So for this adult version we added notes and references to the original booklet as well as suggestions on specific mental exercises.

For anyone who needs to stick a label on the beliefs outlined here, we would say they are based on Humanism, strongly influenced by Stoic ethics[1].

Toronto, 2019

A hard cover version of the 1st edition of this booklet, as well as its iPad ebook counterpart, can be purchased from Blurb Inc.

ebook versions of the 1st edition are available from Amazon's Kindle Store, Apple's iTunes, Google Play Books and Scribd.

The symbol used on the front cover is Leonardo da Vinci's depiction of the 'ideal man', drawn in about 1490 AD. It is commonly referred to as the Vitruvian Man. As you read on, I hope its symbolism will become obvious.

What It Means and How to Do It

What does 'living well' mean?
The moral quality of our lives is determined by the judgments we make and by decisions that often follow. Every decision is a *moral* decision [2], meaning that it is the *right* or *wrong* decision. Some decisions have a huge moral implication, while others not so. Most decisions lead to actions which impact others and the world around us. So, to 'live well' means to habitually make the right judgments, decisions and actions [3].

To understand what 'right' means, we need first to better understand what we are.

What are we?
All of us are individuals, each responsible for the judgments, decisions and actions we make, but we are also part of something much bigger than ourselves. First of all, we have evolved as a part of humanity, and beyond that as part of the biosphere and the cosmos. We are an integral part of everything around us, in the same way that our hands are a part of our bodies. We cannot exist on our own. We depend on things around us, and the things around us depend on us. And we are not only a part of *what is*, but also a part of *what will be*[4]. As such, we have responsibilities towards ourselves, the people we know, the people we don't know, and people yet unborn. And because those people are also part of something bigger – the cosmos – our responsibilities stretch to the cosmos that is and will be.

Evolution and personal excellence
Let's take a look at what we are from the perspective of evolution.

We know that, through the evolutionary process of natural selection, a species can adapt to a constantly changing environment. But the selection process depends on there being genetic differences between members of the species. Nature must have a choice. Genetic diversity is necessary and healthy for the survival of the species. It's good that we differ from each other.

It's good that we don't all look the same [5].

Unfortunately, the environment changes more quickly than the process of genetic adaptation, so if the survival of our species depended only on genetic adaptation, its future would be compromised. Our species would never achieve its full potential and, individually within our species, we could never be the best that we could be - in other words, we could never achieve 'personal excellence' [6].

So while having the right collection of genes is an important component of personal excellence, it's not all. Evolution has also given us a reasoning brain, and it is that reasoning brain that makes up for the 'slowness' of our genes. It is the key to our achieving personal excellence.

Evolution and happiness

Now here is the key point. If you can achieve your full potential, if you can achieve personal excellence, then **you will achieve happiness**. There are many kinds of happiness. The happiness I am writing about is something like tranquility, serenity, being content, the satisfaction that comes from knowing that you are doing the right thing thanks to making the right judgment and the right decision. The closer you get to achieving your full potential, the more often you will experience glimpses of this happiness [7].

So to achieve happiness, you need to work at achieving your full potential. Probably nobody has ever succeeded in getting all the way, but that doesn't matter. What matters is trying and making progress. You can't replace your genes, but you can manage and improve what your genes have given you. You can:

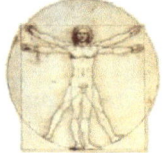

- Care for each part of your body, including your mind (which is just the working brain),
- Care for your body as a whole, understanding that all the parts have to work well together,
- Care for other people, understanding that you are just one part of humanity and all parts have to work well together,
- Care for the cosmos, understanding that humanity is just one part of it and that all parts have to work well together.

If you do this, and only this, you will be as happy as you can possibly be. Happiness is the *reward* that evolution gives you for living up to your full potential.

That's a lot to think about. So let's focus on the brain. After all, that is the one part of the body that controls the whole body, and that gives us the ability to care for humanity and the cosmos. Also, with this remarkable organ, as it has evolved in humans, we can correct the mistakes of nature, the imperfections in our collections of genes, both at the level of the individual and at the level of the human species. It is the mind that allows us to live well as individuals, and it is the mind that gives humanity the ability to survive and prosper.

Managing your mind

'Care for the mind' means: care for the brain and care for how we use it. Like other organs, the brain needs to get the right minerals and chemicals. For that to happen, we need to eat healthily and to exercise our bodies in order to oxygenate the brain (and other organs) [8]. Exercising our brains will help us make the best judgments and decisions more often. But first, how are judgments and decisions made? Let's look at judgments first.

Making the right judgments

All the time our minds are bombarded by impressions, either through the senses, or through conclusions made in various mind processes.

We make judgments, subconscious and conscious, about those impressions. For example:

- Mary looks sexy. If I could have sex with her, I would be really happy!
- A car is about to hit me. I'm going to die!
- My manager is criticizing me. I feel insulted!

Most often, driven by subconscious thoughts [9], we make hasty judgments about the fact (Mary looks sexy; A car is about to hit me; My manager is criticizing me), but instinctively include an immediate emotional response with that judgment (If I could have sex with her, I would be really happy! - *Desire*; I'm going to die! –*Fear*; That's a personal insult! - *Anger*). Other emotions, some of them useful, include disgust, empathy, anxiety, guilt and love.

But in each of the above cases, there are two separate judgments to be made. First, is the fact itself actually true, and what does it mean? Look at the first example. 'Mary looks sexy'. What does that mean? Well, if you pause to think first, your correct judgment may be: 'Yes, she looks sexy. Evolution has created sex appeal for the continuation of the species. But neither she nor I are ready for sex psychologically'. The second judgment, then, should be: 'If we become friends and enjoy each other's company, one day we may be ready for a deeper and more physical relationship'. The result of making two separate judgments is that you stay in control and have a healthy satisfying relationship. But the result of making one judgment followed by an immediate emotional response may be a situation leading to extreme anxiety and other unpleasant consequences.

Unexamined emotional responses attached to subconscious or hasty judgments can be life-savers. However, they can also lead us to make the wrong decisions, possibly followed by the wrong actions. These wrong actions may cause harm to us or to others. In fact, inappropriate emotions are the cause of most of the harmful actions that we ever take [10].

So to make the right judgments, decisions and actions – to live well – you need to constantly challenge your initial judgments about the facts.

As often as you can, after the initial impression: pause and use reason to separate the fact from the emotional response, usually the result of a subconscious judgment (a 'feeling'). Then, use knowledge to judge the reality of the fact itself. Maybe the first emotional response was the right one. But if not, a different and more appropriate response will follow. You will remain calm and cause no harm. This approach, first proposed by Greek

philosophers two thousand years ago [11], is one of the core principles of today's Cognitive Behavioural Therapy (CBT) [12].

Often, you may come to the conclusion that you do not have enough information about the facts to be able to make the judgment. However, you may be able to make use of the judgment of someone you trust, for example a parent or an expert. Then your new judgment will not be about the first impression, but about what trust you can put in the expert.

Suppose you have almost all - but not 100% – of the information you need to make a judgment. Then make a conditional judgment (or 'judgment with reservations'). If you don't apply the condition, you will be in danger of unreasonable expectation and become too attached to the outcome. If a conditional judgment is not possible, suspend judgment altogether.

Making the right decisions

Let's move on to decisions. When attempting to make the *right* decision, you need to consider the impact it may have on your personal self, on others, on the environment, both in the present and in the future. So, a *right* decision is one that is beneficial to you but consistent with your being 'the best that you can be'. And 'the best that you can be' always takes into account what is external to you. **Egoism and altruism are inseparable**.

Sometimes, the decision is easy, because the impact of the decision may obviously be positive on you personally and on what you are a part of. Usually, however, the impact is positive on some things, but negative on others. In this situation, you have to try to make a **balanced** decision that is right for you as an excellent human being. This is called a 'moral dilemma'. There is no simple formula for dealing with every moral dilemma. Each one is unique. When faced with a moral dilemma, do your best in using reason to come up with the right decision, balancing your duties to yourself, to others, and to the environment, in the present and in the future [13].

What you can control and what you can't

Judgments and decisions are the **only** things in your life that are potentially under your complete control [14]. That's because they happen in your mind and your mind only. Your judgments and decisions are usually about external things which are not under your control, such as health, wealth, reputation, physical comfort, words spoken to you, and even past events.

Not only do you have an effect on external things when you make a decision, external things can have an effect on your judgments and decisions – but **only** if you allow them to. For example, if someone attempts to insult you, all they are really doing is using words to get a reaction out of you. They are just words. You can judge that someone is trying to harm you, but you don't have to accept the emotion of a hurt feeling that so often follows. Similarly, if it's bitterly cold, you can experience physical discomfort, but you don't have to be emotionally miserable. **It's up to you!**

Likewise, you can enjoy good health, money, a fine reputation, etc. but you shouldn't get too emotionally attached to them. If you do, then your judgment that you need them will always be followed by an irrational emotional response. For example, if you think your reputation is threatened by someone, you may strike out and hit them - only to find out later that it was the wrong person.

A good test for excessive attachment is what happens when you lose the thing you were attached to. If losing it leads you to misery or despair, your attachment was unreasonable and too strong. **It's up to you!**

Because you can fully control only judgments and decisions, but not actions or their outcomes, **your intentions are more important than the outcomes**.

Evolution has given us the basic tools to distinguish between right and wrong, and has given us a reasoning ability to enable us to use those tools [15]. **The correct use of reason to make judgments and decisions about external things will <u>always</u> produce the morally right result**. It follows that the correct use of reason is the only thing that is unconditionally *good*. External things, at best, can be conditionally good (or bad) depending on how they are used [16].

So now we can return to the meaning of 'right' in the definition of 'living well' given at the beginning of this booklet ('to habitually make the right judgments, decisions and actions'). They are right when they have been arrived at in the right way - through a reasoning process that is completely rational and socially responsible, and that takes all available relevant information and intuitions into account.

Social rules and conventions

Obviously, you can't use reason this way for every decision you make. How many decisions do you make each day? Probably hundreds. So, use your reason for the really important ones, for moral dilemmas and to solve new problems with no precedent. For the rest, there may be social rules you can follow. Where there aren't any or where they are obviously wrong, trust your feelings. Social rules come from cultures overlaying a basic moral code, given to us by evolution, with social conventions developed over thousands of years. As previously mentioned, feelings are the result of subconscious thoughts based on past experiences from which lessons have been learned and stored for future use.

One set of social rules comes from the consideration of 'role duties'. You may be a daughter or son, a student and a citizen. Each of these roles has a set of duties associated with it. For example, as a daughter or son, one of your duties is to respect your parents. As a student, one of your duties is to study well. As a citizen, one of your duties is to obey the law. Think of your role at any time, consider the duties that come with it and your decision will be easier. Another set of rules comes from religions, for example the Ten Commandments in Christianity. Notice that these religions agree about most things. It's wrong to lie, steal, kill or injure yourself and others, be disrespectful, break promises etc. That they agree on so many things is not surprising - the foundation for these things has been built into our nature by evolution.

Use these rules, but be aware that while they are appropriate for most situations, sometimes they are not. Firstly, context is important. What is right in one situation is not right in another. Secondly, they may be influenced by irrational cultural impositions such as women's social inferiority or unconditional loyalty. Thirdly, our knowledge of the cosmos constantly changes. So must our judgments.

Beware of dogma! There are no rules that must be followed in all situations and at all times. You may have to injure someone to save the lives of your family. You may have to lie in order to protect your identity from a dangerous thief. When you have a

doubt as to what is the morally right decision, return to the use of reason. Think for yourself. But if you do, beware of the 'slippery slope'. Reasoning must be **correct reasoning**, which implies – among other things - that it must be honest. It's easy to fool yourself into 'rationalizing' what you wanted anyway. That's **false reasoning** and it's always unconditionally *bad*. Once done, it comes easier next time around, then easier, then easier still... hence the 'slippery slope' analogy.

So how can you improve your ability to reason correctly? Do it by **using your reasoning abilities** at every opportunity, by **practicing appropriate mental exercises** described later on in this booklet and by **developing four essential character traits**: practical wisdom, moderation, courage and justice.

Four Essential Character Traits
Practical Wisdom

Acquire knowledge, and then use that knowledge to make the right decisions. Suspend all prejudices and biases when you do so. Educate yourself continuously, and use reason to apply as much of what you have learned to real life as you can. Plan ahead, choose achievable objectives (ones under your complete control), and then focus on the *here* and *now*.

Moderation

Exercise self-control at all times. Don't get too attached to things you like. Enjoy the things you like, use them well, but remember you don't control them and you may lose them tomorrow. Life will go on. Don't obsess about things you don't like. If you do, your ability to deal with them rationally will be destroyed. Have fun, but never let your emotions get out of control. Be sad when you have to be, but don't let it go on for too long – and never despair.

Courage

Have the guts to do the right thing even when it's unpleasant. Change things for the better if you can. Accept unpleasant truths that can't be changed. Prepare yourself for the unpleasant things that will happen. That will smooth the emotional impact when they do.

Justice

Be sensitive to what is outside of you. Have a keen sense of how your actions impact others, the environment, the present and the future. Behave towards others as you would like them behave towards you (often called the 'Golden Rule') [17]. Work for a better world, in which all are provided with the opportunities to achieve their potential as human beings, as well as the capability of exercising their powers of judgment and decision in selecting from those opportunities [18]. And always remember: sympathy is good (this is how you begin to care for others), empathy is better (you sense what they feel and want to help), rational compassion is best (you develop an emotional distance that allows you to help effectively) [19].

You must develop all four traits[20]. Having less than all four makes it difficult to live well. At worst, having some traits in abundance and lacking others can be dangerous. Hitler, Stalin, Pol Pot and Al Baghdadi all had the courage to take risks to achieve the things they believed in, and were moderate in their personal needs (though they all got addicted to power). But their wisdom was distorted as they could not suspend their prejudices, and their justice was a parody as they lacked compassion.

Egoism and altruism are inseparable. That is how we have evolved. To be happy, you need to care for others. To care for others, you need to care for yourself.

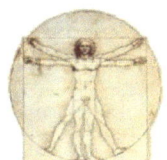

Nine Precepts for Living Well

1. Be hungry for knowledge

2. Be rational in your judgments

3. Be considerate in your decisions

4. Be active in your beliefs

5. Be content with what you cannot change

6. Be controlled in your emotions

7. Be caring for yourself

8. Be moderate in your needs

9. Be compassionate to all

Exercises

Constant exercise is important to the achievement of personal excellence. An unfit or unhealthy body can be an unnecessary burden on society. All the body organs need to be kept in shape, the brain in particular. To function well, the brain needs many nutrients including oxygen. These are delivered to the brain by the flow of blood through the arteries. Physical exercise generally maintains good blood flow, so physical exercise is essential for a healthy brain as well as the rest of the body.

Techniques for exercising the body muscles are well developed, so in this booklet, I will focus on mental exercises. A set of such exercises is proposed here, but you can come up with your own. The concentration and mindfulness exercises have, of necessity, been borrowed and adapted from Eastern traditions where they were best developed.

Ideally, you should exercise every day, preferably early in the morning. Obviously, the amount of exercise you do will depend on your circumstances. There will be times when it goes well, and times when it doesn't. But it is important that you don't get discouraged and that you to get into the habit of exercising, no matter what.

Stoic practices[21]

These exercises will help you internalize the principles of Living Well. They may be most effective if done after the concentration exercises, but will be beneficial if done at any time.

Repetition

> Every day, repeat to yourself the Nine Precepts for Living Well. They are not a mantra. Think about what they mean.

Self-denial and discomfort

> Choose something pleasurable that you planned to do or have today. Deny it to yourself. Alternatively, choose to do something that causes you discomfort (but not harm!).

Control

> Choose an event in which you will participate today. Think about what you want to achieve, what you can control and what you can't. Are there any objectives that you can internalize and bring under your control? Store them in the back of your mind for future use. Now focus on the *here* and *now*.

> Choose an event in which you participated today. What could you have done better? Store your conclusion in the back of your mind for future use. Accept the outcome, no matter how unpleasant. Move on. Focus on the *here* and *now*.

Negative Visualization

> Choose an event that will happen today and whose outcome is important to you. Imagine the worst possible outcome. Then think about how much worse it could be. Think about how you will respond to the various scenarios. Do the same for a longer-term event that you may think of as catastrophic.

Contemplation of Oneness

> In your mind, look at yourself from the outside. Go inwards and imagine your body and all its parts and organs, starting from the top of your head down to your toes. Think of the billions of cells in your body, with old cells constantly dying off and new cells constantly being born. Think of your near-miraculous immune system, with white blood cells of various kinds and antibodies fighting off harmful bacteria and viruses. Imagine too the billions and billions

of good bacteria in your body – living, dying, replicating and keeping your body healthy. Take your mind inside any one of your cells and look at the DNA that is so important to your being that you are.

Now go outwards and imagine yourself as part of your family and your immediate community. See them all as part of the billions of people that make up humanity – all interacting with each other in countless ways. Then reflect on the fact that humanity is only one of millions of species of life on this planet, all dependent on each other. Think of Earth as a biosphere – one organism of which we are a tiny part.

Go even further and imagine Earth as a planet revolving around a star, one of millions in the Orion Arm of the Milky Way galaxy. Then see our galaxy as one of thousands or so making up the Virgo Cluster. Move out further still and imagine a network of billions of clusters and superclusters with voids in between.

Now think of it all as the cosmos which includes its own past and its future. Reflect on where it all might have come from. You came from it and you are a part of it. Every atom you breathe or eat once came from the stars. Over the next year, every atom in your body will return to the biosphere, and eventually the stars. As cosmologist Carl Sagan said, "Our planet, our society, and we ourselves are built of star stuff."

Concentration[22]

This exercise will help you focus and calm you down.

Sit upright on a chair (not an armchair!) and start breathing naturally with your mouth slightly open.

As you breathe, in your mind count to ten with each in-out breath and then continue on, thinking to yourself "in" and "out" as you breathe in and out. Focus your awareness on the sensation of your breath. Do not think about it; just be aware of the sensation.

As, inevitably, stray thoughts do interrupt, put them aside non-judgmentally and return your awareness to your breath. If stray thoughts are particularly disruptive, return to counting to ten. The ability to breathe ten times without disruption will be an important milestone in your progress.

During the first month, do this for 10 minutes. Afterwards, increase the time for each session by five minutes each month – until you reach forty-five minutes.

At the beginning, stray thoughts will interrupt you immediately and continuously. That's OK. After some months, you may be able to achieve uninterrupted concentration periodically. This is called 'access concentration'. During such periods, you will still be aware of background sensations and you may feel happiness, see flashes of light, feel your body floating apart and even see visions. Ignore them and continue focusing on your breath.

Eventually, perhaps after a year or two, you may reach a state in which you can achieve immediate and long-lasting uninterrupted concentration effortlessly. This is called 'full absorption'. There will be no disruptive thoughts and no bodily sensations.

Mindfulness[23]

This exercise will help you focus and improve emotional self-discipline by separating the emotion from the judgment.

After you have achieved access concentration or full absorption, focus your mind on bodily sensations, feelings and emotions as they arise, and not exclusively on your breathing. As each of these arises, recognize it by giving it a name, and put it aside while letting other sensations recede into the background.

When you are able to do this without interruption, proceed to 'choiceless awareness' by expanding awareness to include simultaneously all sensations, feelings and emotions – and letting your mind free.

As with concentration, as you continue on, you may pass through various levels of insight. If you do, be sure to use reason either to give your assent to them (i.e. judge them to be true) or to reject them.

Endnotes and References

[1] 'Humanism' is defined by the American Humanist Association as 'a progressive philosophy of life that, without supernaturalism, affirms our ability and responsibility to lead ethical lives of personal fulfillment that aspire to the greater good of humanity'. But why does personal fulfillment imply working for the greater good of humanity? How does one lead to the other? For many humanists, the connection is intuitively obvious, but it is the ethics teachings of Stoicism that provide reasons for the *why* and the *how*.

The Stoic school of philosophy was founded in Athens around 300 BC by Zeno of Citium (now Larnaca in Cyprus), and eventually found many adherents in the Greek and Roman worlds. But as a philosophy that encourages people to think for themselves, it was not convenient for Roman Emperor Justinian who needed a state religion, Christianity, that he could control. He persecuted all other religions and philosophies. Justinian closed all the Greek philosophy schools in 529 AD. Stoicism was 'rediscovered' thanks to Muslim Arab philosophers such as Al-Kindi (801-873 AD) who translated the works of the Greek philosophers into Arabic and enabled their re-introduction into medieval Europe through the Muslim occupation of Spain and Portugal.

Stoicism has left its mark on today's Western culture through pre-Enlightenment and Enlightenment philosophers, thinkers and statesmen such as Adam Burski (Poland, 1560 – 1611 AD), René Descartes (France, 1596 – 1650AD), Baruch Spinoza (Holland, 1632 – 1677 AD), John Locke (England, 1632– 1704 AD), Adam Smith (Scotland, 1723 – 1790 AD), Emmanuel Kant (Prussia/Germany, 1724 – 1804 AD) and George Washington (USA, 1732 – 1799 AD).

It's worth noting that although the ancient classical Stoics were theists, their ethical teachings did not require a belief in supernatural power. Stoic Roman Emperor Marcus Aurelius (121 – 180 AD) wrote: 'Live a good life. If there are gods and they are just, then they will not care how devout you have been, but will welcome you based on the virtues you have lived by. If there are gods, but unjust, then you should not want to worship them. If there are no gods, then you will be gone, but will have lived a noble life that will live on in the memories of your loved ones'. For a more comprehensive description of Stoicism, read *A Little Book of Stoicism* by

St. George Stock or *Stoicism* by John Sellars.

[2] But what about the hundreds if not thousands of 'trivial' decisions we make every day? For example, suppose I need to decide what I should use to write a letter. Should I use a pencil or a ball-point pen? How can that be a moral decision? Well consider some questions you could ask yourself in making it?

- What is the carbon footprint in the manufacture of each of the two options?
- With forests in decline, but needed to absorb excess carbon dioxide from the atmosphere, should we be using anything made of wood if alternatives are available?
- Once discarded, won't the plastic pen lie around forever – polluting the environment for future generations?
- With a young child in the house, should I have sharp pencils lying around when there are safer alternatives available?

The likely impact of this decision may be small, but like every decision, it does have a moral dimension.

[3] Here, 'judgments' includes opinions and beliefs. 'Decisions' are intentions to take action and always involve choice. At the very least, a choice is to act or not to act. Here, 'decisions' means real decisions, ones followed by a solid commitment to carry them through, provided the facts on which they were based have not changed. 'Actions' may or may not result in their intended outcomes, and should not be confused with them.

[4] Zeno, who became the first head of the Stoic school, and the early Stoics believed that the cosmos is one organic 'whole'. Stoic philosopher Posidonius of Apameia (135 – 51 BC) later developed the idea of 'cosmic sympathy' – meaning that all parts of the cosmos are interconnected and therefore interdependent. Marcus Aurelius wrote in *Meditations* about the psychological importance of seeing oneself and other human beings as parts of one great organism.

Buddhists and Taoists also believe that all things exist only in relationship to one another.

Science has already shown how we interact within and with the biosphere. The exact nature of our interaction with the rest of the cosmos has yet to be determined by future scientists.

Living Well

The following is Article 28 of *The Constitution of the Iroquois Nations*: 'Look and listen for the welfare of the whole people and have always in view not only the present but also the coming generations, even those whose faces are yet beneath the surface of the ground, the unborn of the future Nation'.

[5] For a modern and readable description of the theory of natural selection, first formulated by naturalist Charles Darwin in *The Origin of the Species* (1809 – 1882 AD), read *The Selfish Gene* by Oxford University evolutionary biologist Richard Dawkins (1941 AD -).

Biologist E.O. Wilson (1929 AD -) of Harvard University has proposed how natural selection results in our caring for future generations.

[6] Zeno stated that the goal of life should be 'to live according to Nature' (sometimes phrased: 'to live as Nature intended').

To better understand how this relates to personal excellence, let's take a look at what we know today about the human body, as described by Daniel. E. Lieberman (1964 AD -), Professor of Biological Sciences at Harvard University, in *The Story of the Human Body*. The human body evolved from its primitive origins for millions of years, constantly adapting through natural selection to an ever-changing environment. About 10,000 years ago, it had adapted almost perfectly to its environment as the body of a hunter-gatherer. In its quest for food and safety, it was capable of intense physical activity. It consumed a diverse diet of fruits, tubers, seeds, nuts, wild game and other foods that are rich in fibre and vitamins but low in sugar. It had also evolved a new part of the brain – the neocortex – that allowed it to reason for the purposes of planning and cooperating with others. However, since then, genetically, it has not evolved very much. There hasn't been enough time. Our genes and our brain size are basically those of the hunter-gatherer (although there must have been some biological changes in the brain: the number of inter-neural connections has probably increased). Yet our lifestyle has changed. Most of us sit more than we walk, farm our food, and eat lots of sugars, processed grains and processed meats from domesticated animals. But our bodies have not had the time to adapt to this new lifestyle. We are, generally, no longer living according to Nature. Clearly, to live 'as Nature intended', we need to exercise our bodies more, eat food for which our bodies are best adapted, and use correct reason to solve the challenges of life. If we manage to do that, our bodies and minds will do what evolution 'designed' them to do and we will achieve personal excellence.

Zeno used observation and logic to arrive at much the same conclusion, though he focused on how best to use the most important organ – the brain. He stated that each living entity should stay close to Nature by trying to live as the best example of its species. For the human species, that is unique in its ability to use reason, the best example is a 'sage'. A sage has perfected the use of judgments and decisions. She never makes a mistake – because, to begin with, she recognizes the difference between certainty and uncertainty. In the case of certainty, she always makes the correct judgment given the knowledge available. In the case of uncertainty, she will either make a conditional judgment or suspend it altogether. Because she never makes a false judgment, and because uncontrolled emotions are the result of false judgments about what is good and what is bad, she has complete mastery of her emotions. By focusing on the perfection of her inner self, she is able to engage more appropriately and effectively with the outside world. She has achieved personal excellence – the ultimate form of humanism's concept of personal fulfillment. Stoicism makes us better humanists.

[7] In Stoic philosophy, this happiness is referred by the ancient Greek word 'eudaimonia'. What that meant exactly was and still is a subject of debate. Today, we know that the human body produces many hormones that contribute to our feeling 'good'. For example, dopamines contribute to a feeling of intense euphoria. Endorphins give feeling of comfortable calmness by reducing pain. Oxytocin is clearly related to feelings of trust, empathy, affection and love. In fact, the many ways that these hormones can act and interact results in an almost infinite number of ways we can feel happy, and in each of us experiencing unique forms of happiness. But despite the difficulty of defining the precise mechanisms of happiness, we all know about how good we feel when we know that we have done the 'right thing'. Also, it does seem intuitively obvious that evolution, through the process of natural selection, would use the mechanism of happiness to reward behaviours that result in the survival of our species.

[8] Neurologist Dr. David Perlmutter in *Grain Brain* (published in 2013) describes how both exercise and diet can affect DNA – specifically how it can switch on certain genes to produce protein BDNF (brain-derived neurotrophic factor) which protects neurons and helps produce new neurons and synapses. He also points out that the brain uses 20% of the body's energy. If not looked after, the brain can literally be starved of

energy and permanently damaged.

[9] Science journalist Jonah Lehrer (1981 AD -) in *How We Decide*, writes this explanation of subconscious thinking: 'Essentially your impression is first subconsciously evaluated against a database of past judgments and outcomes that have been stored for all time, and result in emotions and feelings. This process that has been fine-tuned over eons is fast and voluminous. Conscious thinking is slow and can only deal with a small number of variables at a time. Use rational thinking to decide if more analysis is realistic or if we should trust our feelings'.

Our database of past judgments and outcomes is constantly changing and being added to. That database is a part of our memories. Cognitive psychologist Elizabeth Loftus (1944 AD -) and others have shown that our memories are constantly being re-interpreted and re-written. Memories that we would swear are accurate can be false memories. False memories lead to false judgments.

It is clear that while our conscious thinking must be the final judge of what judgments and decisions are true or false, we need both the conscious and the sub-conscious parts of our minds to work together in order to flourish. This is what Lebanese poet Khalil Gibran (1863 – 1931 AD) wrote in *The Prophet*: 'Your reason and your passion are the rudder and the sails of your seafaring soul. If either your sails or your rudder be broken, you can but toss and drift, or else be held at a standstill in mid-seas. For reason, ruling alone, is a force confining; and passion, unattended, is a flame that burns to its own destruction. Therefore let your soul exalt your reason to the height of passion that it may sing. And let it direct your passion with reason that your passion may live through its own daily resurrection and, like the Phoenix, rise above its own ashes.'

[10] Early Stoic philosophers believed that all emotions (including desire/attachment) are the result of faulty judgments about what is good and what is bad, and therefore unnatural. Later Stoic philosophers Panaetius of Rhodes (185 BC – 110 BC) and Posidonius stated that emotions are natural, but should be ruled by reason. Modern Stoic philosopher Lawrence Becker (1939 AD -) in *The New Stoicism* takes this further by saying that reason should be used to appropriately apportion attachment to objects, but never in a way that obstructs our ability to do the right thing. In other words, excessive attachment is obsession.

According to Duke University philosopher David B. Wong in 'The

Meaning of Detachment in Taoism, Buddhism, and Stoicism' (in *Dao: A Journal of Comparative Philosophy*), Buddhists and Taoists also come to the same conclusion and advocate the cultivation of detachment.

But where do negative emotions come from? How did they evolve? According to cosmologist Carl Sagan (1934 – 1996 AD) in *The Dragons of Eden*, negative emotions may be the result of conflicts between different parts of our brain that evolved at different times – the reptilian complex (aggression, territoriality, social hierarchies), the limbic or mammalian system (passions, altruism etc) and the neocortex (consciousness, memory, imagination, planning, deliberation, abstract thinking, creative thinking, non-verbal intuition, judgment, decision making etc). These negative emotions served our ancestors well, but may no longer be needed in their original form. For example, fear was necessary for cavemen to save them from sabre-toothed tigers. Today, our lives are much safer, but those primal instincts are still there, hidden deeply inside our brains in their original form and intensity.

The different parts of our brain are constantly communicating with each other. One part, the orbitofrontal cortex (OFC), mediates between the limbic system and the neocortex by sending information about emotional states and feelings from the limbic system to the dorsolateral prefrontal cortex (DLPFC) in the neocortex. There a decision can be made as to whether they should be inhibited or acted on.

Another part, the anterior cingulate cortex (ACC), is key to our subconscious learning and adapting to new facts as they are processed by the DLPFC. When dopamine neurons (responsible for the production of intense feelings) in the limbic system detect errors - disagreements between our feelings/intuitions and what actually happened - they stop producing dopamine. The ACC stores this information for future use, and also transmits it to the DLPFC so as to enable better decisions. In this way, the brain learns from past mistakes. Our subconscious mind absorbs information from our rational mind and allows for more dependable intuitions and feelings in the future.

Negative emotions can also arise from chemical imbalances in the brain. Provided one's ability to reason is not physically damaged, they can be dealt with cognitively by, for example, CBT (Cognitive Behavioural Therapy). Where cognitive therapies don't work on their own, they may be supplemented by drugs that attempt to restore the brain's chemical balance

– though these can result in unwelcome side effects. For the story of how someone coped with one negative emotion, serious depression, after losing her job, read *Out of the Blue* by journalist Jan Wong (1952 - AD).

[11] Chryssipus of Soli (279 – 206 BC), the third head of the Stoic school of philosophy, systematized and expanded Zeno's doctrines. It was probably he who first developed this approach to managing the relationship between impressions, assents (judgments as to whether the impressions are true) and emotions.

Our ability to make a bad situation worse by assenting without thinking, and suffering the emotional consequence, is the subject of some notable quotes:

> "Man is disturbed not by things, but by the views he takes of them".(Epictetus - see endnote 14)
>
> "Get rid of judgment, get rid of the 'I am hurt' and you will be rid of the hurt itself". (Marcus Aurelius)
>
> "The mind is its own place, and in itself can make a heaven of hell, and a hell of heaven". (Milton's Satan)
>
> "There's nothing good or bad but thinking makes it so". .(Shakespeare's Hamlet)
>
> "No one can make you feel inferior without your consent". (Eleanor Roosevelt)

Austrian neurologist Sigmund Freud (1856 – 1939 AD) developed the idea that the way to finally get rid of negative emotions is to indulge in them. Even today, many people believe that you can get rid of anger by thrashing a punch bag while pretending it is the object of their anger. In fact, scientific experiments have shown the opposite to be true. Indulging in negative emotions tends to increase them. For more on this read *Does Venting Anger Feed or Extinguish the Flame?* by Ohio State University psychologist Brad Bushman.

[12] For the connection between CBT and the Stoics, read *The Philosophy of Cognitive-Behavioural Therapy (CBT)* by psychologist Donald Robertson.

[13] How to balance duties was addressed by Roman philosopher Cicero (106–43 BC) in *On Duties*, and probably derived from the teachings of Panaetius (185 – 110 BC), the seventh head of the Stoic school.

Each of us, as an individual, has a hierarchy of many identities. They naturally fall into four identity categories:

> *1. The Universal*
>
> The identity of the human being, that which should be common to us all. Characteristic: A completely rational social being.
>
> *2. The Personal*
>
> The identity of each of us imposed by nature; the combination of qualities that makes each of us unique. Characteristic: Compared to other human beings, nature may have made you tall or small, exceptionally good or bad at math, male or female or transgender, serious or flippant, fast or slow, introverted or extroverted, etc.
>
> *3. The Circumstantial*
>
> The identities of each of us imposed by circumstance. Characteristic: You may be someone born in a country at war or in a country at peace, a citizen of Uruguay or a stateless refugee, or witness to a crime or its victim.
>
> *4. The Chosen*
>
> The identities that each of us has chosen following a series of judgments and decisions. Characteristic: You may be a business consultant or a social worker, a parent or a single, a football player or a coin collector.

Each of these identities provides us with a role in life. If we are to achieve personal excellence then we need to make appropriate judgments and decisions so as to fulfill each and all of these roles in the best possible way. This is what is sometimes referred to as one's role duty. But what if there is a conflict between role duties? Then the hierarchy of duties provides us with a resolution. Each role duty must be subject to higher level role duties. The higher level always trumps the lower level. For example, if you choose to be a competition basketball player, is that in accordance with the fact that you happen to be smaller than average and have poor ball-handling skills? Clearly your Chosen Identity would be in conflict with your Personal Identity. You may get pleasure from playing, but you may let the team down. Possibly, it would be wrong to become a basketball player. If you had chosen to be a Nazi judge in Germany in 1940, would that have been in accordance with your being a rational social human being? You may claim that you *chose* to be a judge, but that to be a Nazi was *imposed* on you by Hitler. But either way, your Chosen Identity or your Circumstantial Identity would have been in conflict with your Universal Identity. It would have been wrong to be a Nazi judge.

[14] According to his pupil Flavius Arrion, Stoic teacher Epictetus (55 – 135 AD), a Greek slave in the Roman Empire, made it clear that this is the key to living a tranquil life. The opening lines in his *Enchiridion(Handbook)* are 'Some things are up to us and some are not up to us. Things in our complete control are opinion, pursuit, desire, aversion, and, in a word, whatever are our own actions. Things not in our complete control are body, property, reputation, command, and, in one phrase, whatever are not our own actions '. Earlier, Cicero used the concept of the Perfect Archer to demonstrate what really matters: The ideal, according to him, was 'to hit the centre of the target, though accomplishing this is not entirely in the archer's power, for she cannot be certain how the wind will deflect the arrow from its path, nor whether her fingers will slip, nor whether (for it is within the bounds of possibility) the bow will break. The excellent archer does all within her power to shoot well, and she recognizes that doing her best is the best she can do. The Stoic archer strives to shoot excellently, and will not be disappointed if she shoots well but fails to hit the centre of the target.'

[15] We know that Epictetus believed that we are born with an innate conception of what is good and what is bad. In *Enchiridion*, he states: "Every one of us, slave or free, has come into this world with innate conceptions as to 'good' or 'bad', 'noble' and 'shameful'...'fitting' and 'inappropriate'."

In our age, the investigation of how morality depends on evolution is a new field of study. Evolutionary biologist Marc D. Hauser (1959 AD -) in *Moral Minds* suggests that a gene or a combination of genes provides a basic template for determining right and wrong (e.g. to kill is wrong...). The template is modified by cultural customs (e.g...except in self-defence).

Living Well

Psychologist and philosopher Patricia Churchland (1943 AD -) in her book *Braintrust* believes that morality grows out of empathy, and that the 'trust/love' hormone oxytocin is key to this process. She states: "Morality seems to be a natural phenomenon – constrained by the forces of natural selection, rooted in neurobiology, shaped by the local ecology, and modified by cultural development." So, although we can arrive rationally at the idea that we have a duty towards others, it's good to know that our conclusion is supported by our genes.

[16] It was ancient Greek philosopher Socrates (469 – 399 BC), a forerunner of the Stoics whose teachings inspired Zeno to become a philosopher, who said that the only real good is wisdom. Everything else is either good or bad depending on how it is used. Later, the Stoics refined this understanding of 'wisdom' to mean 'the use of reason'.

[17] Yet even this rule, found in so many religions, must be subject to reason. It does not work well 100% of the time in 100% of situations. For example, you may be relatively indifferent to people calling you names. Does that mean you can call other people names whenever you feel like it? They are probably not sages and may be more sensitive than you. They may be hurt by what you say, and may even become embittered and take it out on others.

[18] Stoic philosopher Hierocles (about 150 AD -) provided this description of how we should behave not only towards members of our immediate family, but also those beyond: 'Each one of us is, as it were, entirely encompassed by many circles, some smaller, others larger, the latter enclosing the former on the basis of their different and unequal dispositions relative to each other. The first and closest circle is the one which a person has draws as though around a centre, his own mind. This circle encloses the body and anything taken for the sake of the body. For it is virtually the smallest circle, and almost touches the centre itself. Next, the second one further removed from the centre but enclosing the first circle; this contains parents, siblings, wife, and children. The third one has in it uncles and aunts, grandparents, nephews, nieces, and cousins. The next circle includes the other relatives, and this is followed by the circle of local residents, then the circle of fellow tribesmen, next that of fellow citizens, and then in the same way the circle of people from neighbouring towns, and then the circle of fellow-countrymen. The outermost and largest circle, which encompasses all the rest, is that of the whole human race. Once these have all been surveyed, it is the task of a well-tempered

person, in his proper treatment of each group, to draw the circles together somehow towards the centre, and to keep zealously transferring those from the enclosing circles into the enclosed ones. It is incumbent on us to respect people from the third circle as if they were those from the second, and again to respect our other relatives as if they were those from the third circle'.

Justice, then, is about the duty of morally correct behaviour towards others, both at the individual level and at the level of society. As social beings, we should be active in promoting conditions in which everyone can achieve personal excellence and live well.

> Firstly, everyone should have the opportunity to learn to think rationally and to take responsibility for their judgments and decisions. This implies an educational system that teaches critical thinking and encourages personal choice and responsibility at an early age. Furthermore, mental health services should have a greater presence within the wider health services system.

> Secondly, everyone should have the knowledge to which they can apply their critical thinking abilities. This implies easy access for everyone to the world's store of knowledge (e.g. internet, libraries, knowledge-focused media, transparency in governance etc).

> Thirdly, everyone should have the freedom to exercise their abilities to judge, make decisions and act accordingly. This implies democracy in politics, the right to opt out of national programs provided there is no negative impact on those who opt in, and respect for opinions in the workplace and at home.

> Fourthly, everyone should have the conditions for making correct judgments and decisions. This implies a minimum degree of: physical and economical security, good health and self-esteem.

With regard to the role of government, it follows from the above that ultimately a just society is one that fosters the intellectual and physical development of each of its citizens by providing appropriate resources and conditions. In this view, gross national product is merely a means to achieve an end, not the end itself.

For a theory of justice that supports the above conclusions, read *Creating Capabilities* by philosopher Martha C. Nussbaum (1947 AD -).

But, note the difference between a just society based on the concept of codified human rights (HR) and one based on our duties to others. Steve Marquis in *International Stoic Forum – Yahoo Group March 13, 2007* writes: 'In an HR-based society both the donor and donee will be devastated if the aid effort fails. The donor had an emotional investment and the donee felt an entitlement. In the duties-based society, neither will be disappointed. The donor did his best, the donee didn't feel entitled. Feeding citizens on the sugar water of entitlement of HR will disenfranchise them from further moral development where responsibility is central.'

[19] 'Rational compassion' here means an emotional need to help, but tempered by reason. If, for example, mothers were guided by the emotional component alone, then their babies would never learn to walk, as their mothers would attempt to alleviate their offspring's emotional stress by picking them up immediately when they got into trouble. The child would never learn to walk by itself.

[20] This is also known as 'The Unity of the Virtues'. It was an important element of Stoic teachings, addressed by Chryssipus, and probably Zeno before him. In Becker's *New Stoicism*, this principle is called 'the integration of agency'. Some people consider all four traits to be aspects of the one virtue of wisdom.

[21] For more on Stoic exercises, read *A Guide to the Good Life* by philosopher William B. Irvine and Appendix 1, The Philosophy of Cognitive-Behavioural Therapy (CBT) by psychologist Donald Robertson.

[22] This is based on Samatha meditation as practiced in Theravada Buddhism.

For more on concentration exercises, read *Pneuma, Will Power Meditation* by Stoic Erik Wiegardt, and chapter 8 (2) in *Meditation: The Buddhist Way of Tranquility and Insight* by Buddhist teacher Kamalashila (Anthony Matthews). Note that in Eastern traditions, concentration and mindfulness are steps on the way to accessing our subconscious and achieving 'insight'. If by doing these exercises you do achieve what seem to be insights, be sure to examine and judge them rationally before giving them your assent.

[23] This is based on Vipassana meditation as practiced in Theravada Buddhism.

For more on mindfulness exercises, read chapter Sitting Meditation in *Coming to Our Senses* by MIT molecular biologist John Kabat-Zinn.

www.ingramcontent.com/pod-product-compliance
Lightning Source LLC
Chambersburg PA
CBHW041819040426
42452CB00004B/154